salmonpoetry

Diverse Voices from Ireland and the World

SUSAN RICH

Gallery of Postcards and Maps

New &
Selected Poems

Published in 2022 by
Salmon Poetry
Cliffs of Moher, County Clare, Ireland
Website: www.salmonpoetry.com
Email: info@salmonpoetry.com

ISBN 978-1-915022-13-4

Cover Image: "Caravan, 1955" by Remedios Varo, reproduced with the permission of the artist's estate and the Artists Rights Society

Front Cover design: *Angelia Miranda and Patheresa Wells*
Back Cover Design & Book Typesetting: *Siobhán Hutson*

Printed in Ireland by Sprint Print

One has to be careful what one takes when one goes away forever

[…] there are many different magics—

LEONORA CARRINGTON

For traveling poets near and far

and for my students

INTRODUCTION

Susan Rich's journey to poetry is quite different from most of her contemporaries. It is rooted in her work on behalf of human rights in Bosnia and Herzegovina, Gaza, South Africa, the Republic of Niger, and elsewhere. I begin with this not to say that such work is necessary for one to become a poet, but to say that her experience in the larger world has impacted Susan Rich's sensibilities. Her perspectives, tonalities, imagery, and choice of subjects are all rooted in a way she learned to observe things, in her understanding that "journeys do not happen in straight lines".

Journeys don't happen in straight lines. Well, neither do poems.

Whether lyrics or narratives, songs or incantations, travelogues or rites, the lines always lead inward. This balance between her attentiveness to the larger world, and her alertness to the inner space of the lyric poem, is what interests me in Susan Rich's work.

*

Her first book, *The Cartographer's Tongue*, offered us a kind of travelogue: the lyrical impressions were passed on the reader in clear moments, images, epiphanies. When this kind of poem works, the author's journey to a particular city becomes a reader's discovery or new ability to articulate something in their own day. This works best when detail and abstraction come together, producing the texture of language that's compelling. For instance, something like this:
"The train.../pulls the weight of wind, of ostriches and coal;/stitches the empty pockets of small towns, /...of the psalms."

When she published her first book, most of Rich's contemporaries didn't write political poems. Surely, Adrienne Rich, Denise Levertov, Carolyn Forché were all at work, and produced powerful lyric poems. Surely, Allen Ginsberg was still reciting *Howl* to packed auditoriums and Gwendolyn Brooks and Lucille Clifton were already much beloved and honored elders. Still, the kind of intense participation in the public discourse that we see among younger poets today wasn't really a thing for most poets of Rich's generation at that time.

But any reader of Rich's early books will find her already leaning in this direction: she is drawing the connective line between mere political argument and daily life, she is showing via imagery, via line-breaks, that all decisions we make are impacting the world we live in.

The names and subtitles of many of those early poems speak for themselves: Sarajevo, Haiti, Niger. But it is not just her perspective that interests me here. It is the vividness of Susan Rich's images, the experience of immediate details that I am drawn to. Take for instance these lines about the women in Vitez, Bosnia:

> It is the best watermelon in the world
> but there's no way to say it in words.
>
> She had squatted in the space for apples and pears
> under the staircase, a year, beyond the place of words.
>
> Now she comes back with tea, examines me closely,
> my out-of-date phrase book, my mispronounced words.
>
> I ask for the toilet and she shows me the bedrooms, bombed
> by neighbors who should have known how to use words.
>
> We walk out to her garden in late afternoon light,
> survey squash plants and corn stalks, we re-enter words.
>
> In Bosnia, the tomato is called paradise (…).

Here, Susan Rich makes no secret of the fact that she is a stranger in that world, often a visitor into the suffering of others—but because she is honest about this, without a trace of pretension, because she is there not for fun but real life work ("the ordinariness of / townships, / truth commissions"), her perspective adds to the larger texture, her language adds to the tonal variation, urgency.

These early poems take her all over, say, to the very powerful scene depicted in the piece called *Women of Kismayo*, or to Gaza City, where Susan Rich marvels at how "all men wear mustaches / which decorate their faces / in soft curved designs//...So many mustaches! Such strange lands!" But with all this exclamation, also comes an acute sense of pain ("Yes, we had losses. // The local correspondent in Zvornick, / our finance clerk traveling between offices.") which turns into a metaphysics:

Whatever happens to the bodies still alive?
Whatever exuberance may they hold?
Whatever dies returns to be retold.

Now, years later, one still finds this reaching out towards the larger world, even in the most unpredictable and wonderfully playful (in their textures of domestic and intimate observations) new poems: there is still that leaning towards the "radio frequency," still a "mind moving like cloudscape," still a metaphysical questioning about "what compels us from our houses / during the pandemic / to wonder and stroll and skate".

But there are also some distinct changes: decades had passed. We have a chance to see the poet develop, grow, sometimes even in ways she or her readers could never have anticipated. There is, for instance, that complete delight and sweetness and playfulness of poems such as *Food for Fallen Angels*. There is also a new meditative tone of very lovely pieces such as *Facing 50 with a Line by Robert Hayden* and *The Self*. There is that unexpected, but altogether welcome surrealist bow in pieces such as *Blue Grapes*. There is, too, a wonderful blend of portrait and dwelling—almost metaphysical, and yet very real—in pieces such as *Tricks a Girl Can Do*. There is also that "extreme close-up," a wise moment of looking at a face and observing "wonderment" is "hooked to sorrow". There is, too, that ability of looking at the eyes and seeing "screams in a sky / of whipped egg whites".

All of that, yes. A life-long journey through poems. But wait, even here, years later, the poet still tells us: "All the things I love […] come from movement." She is still on a road, isn't she?

But of course, we knew that: we knew that the journeys do not happen in straight lines, from A to Z, we knew that the poet must go from one tonality to another, and at times burst into several different tonalities at once. That is how new perspectives come to us.

That's what Susan Rich does so well in this book: she is a poet who can be both solitary and worldly, meditative, and playful. She is a poet who will offer many a journey, all of which will be yours as soon as you turn this page.

—ILYA KAMINSKY

Table of Contents

from—THE ALCHEMIST'S KITCHEN (2010)

from—CLOUD PHARMACY (2014)

New Poems
CARAVAN OF DOVES

Every Clock is Made of Foxes

At midnight, the harvest moon bothers my sleep
and I wake early for my class in Java and Swift—

the exact second when this barking fox
under my bunk shows her cubs, dimpled

and smelling of cherries doused in cream.
The telephone wings circles

around us, sending messages of apology
to the wisteria vine, which does not answer.

The mother fox warns of a cyber-attack,
calling me in a secret name known

only to the Idaho potatoes, which look out
of so many eyes they become academics.

The clock drops minutes and cries after them,
the calendar tears a page from the ocean:

Reward for Lost Time. I search the sands
of the hourglass for a Tuesday gone late August,

track down two presidential terms.
The phone blinks again and the foxes

murmur their timeless faces to the moon.
I must change my life.

Pomegranate, Radio On

Begin with the fruit in your hands—
hold the weight of its rough skin,
its nested, cell interior.

Take your time.

Choose a lilac
blue bowl and pull your sharpest knife
from the cutlery drawer.

This has become your life, not the headlines

but the fine print
of the back pages.
Read slowly the small, good

stories—each image, other worldly.

You're here
at the sink caressing—
there's no other word—

until surreal tomorrows extend—

beyond sustenance, beyond juice,
stained fingers, stained news—

Song at the End of the Mind

I think of you as a radio frequency—
sometimes hard to find

as I touch the illuminated dial.
But tonight you arrive

murmuring into my ear in halfsleep;

you offer a suitcase of longings
and laughter that somersaults its way across the country.

In this time of shelter in place,
we are fevered wanderers

with nothing but an open screen;

handheld devices offering luminous ellipses.
We heal the earthquaked bones

of our pasts decorating rough mouths
with new vocabularies—

no longer deferred.

As the world quiets,
I'm awake to our longings.

All that is left: to congregate
close along the shoreline

unbandaged and unadorned;

to listen to the smooth rhythm and blues
of Quarantine Radio.

This one goes out to you.

For the first time I am afraid

of my country, I say, and he says,
yes. He who has not

taken his safety for granted
does not shame me

for only understanding this now.
We navigate the broken

interstate, eyes focused on
our near-future and the shape

of the conversation continues on
in slow-drawn twists and turns—

past green exit signs and a floating
bridge that disappears across the lake,

behind the cut—two complete
strangers drawn in black and in white—

driving our nation's highways
in the rush hour of late spring.

Dear Wild Unknown

Today you wander towards me through the apocalyptic
newsrooms and by the glow of backlit smart screens.

For you, we have emptied our schools, shuttered

the cafes, prohibited picnics by the sea. Today, I trust
only the unsettled cloudscape,

the fleeting mission of cherry blossoms

lined up here on 47th Street. Like everyone,
I overthink the fever burn of skin, the dry brush

at the back of the throat—a whole expressway

of sensations that travel through our bodies.
Dear Wild Unknown, you whom I so often adored,

looked-up to in an extended outlook of bright constellations.

You whom I've courted and worked to construct
in the lit room of a stanza.

Deep within the intimate feel of this pen,

you seduced with syllables—my friend with benefits.
But not now. Now you've emptied the greengrocers of Venice,

the local playgrounds, and my own first date at Vivacé's—

all indefinitely postponed. Instead, I venture out
to the neighborhood pharmacy, the lonely shelves—

no hand sanitizer in the land. Dear, Dear Unknown—

tell me what can we do with our bodies
now that we cannot hold hands?

I stand on the back porch and practice

my cracked aria rising up through the alleyway
as in Verona but unfortunately,

we Americans are not born singers, instead we howl

and bang pots. What can we do but cry out
onto the page? Scratch a code in curved lines and dashes—

imagining the day we will reclaim our own good names.

Caravan of One

for Remedios Varo

Better than an orgasm: your own traveling cathedral
of piano blues and midnight luminescence—a man lifting

you away from the quiet need for a paycheck, the tiresome
chat-ups with ad execs. Better than multiple orgasms:

creating your own composition in a land of androgenous beings—
the wind-powered bicycle lords obscured, to the left, applauding.

Your amorous impulses transform into a night of fog-lit paths,
driven miles by someone whose face remains carefully masked.

Female or male, orgasms arrive much the same. Is art
masculine or feminine? Highbrow or low?

A caravan of one moves into the almost dark
rushing past spectacular lovers that you took lying down—

or were you the liar? Perhaps. The autonomous fearless flyer:
cigarettes, cats, and canvases were all you ever desired.

Self Portrait as Gustav Courbet

after The Desperate Man, 1843

Just outside the frame Courbet observes a child
languishing in a cage along the border,
like a zoo animal badly neglected; he sees a man
left to bleed out on a St. Louis downtown street;
witnesses a woman at home, killed by Seattle police.
Iridescent terror singed with a bent tuning fork
of truth is how the world enters him: he paints
with sable brush and silvered mirror. The forehead
lit from the inside like a postmodern mind on fire.
His skin, a color not found in nature—except
in the aftermath of gunshot wounds or off a smoked prism
from a chandelier. His eyes: two screams in a sky
of whipped egg whites—beyond open, beyond woke—
as if he's locked to the horizon of this decade and dare not look away.

Secret Agent

A long-armed monkey lurks by the far
edge of the table, a kind of night watchman
half-hidden behind lace tablecloths,

his tail an upside-down question mark.

Naked, of course, and disinclined
to join the party.
I think of your life this way, Leonora—observer

of other realms—holed-up like a secret agent
with the oddest of binoculars—
your gaze that of professor, or perhaps an undertaker.

How you hated your coming out party—
you said it was like your father selling a product—

and not one he believed in.
How your teachers complained—often—
Leonora does not collaborate well.

Wild animal, the headmistress hissed

as you left her wallpapered rooms
for the next.

You would recall with distaste
weekends of flowing cocktails, offered
by strangers with odd-shaped heads—

the food laid out as some anemic image

of the afterlife. You'd disappeared by then—
self-appointed linguist at the local zoo,
each day meeting with Lesula monkeys, African hyenas,

to learn their languages, to paint their gorgeous minds.

What If a House?

The house grows wild, floats
one eyeball above the roofline.

The backdoor listens to nimbus clouds
and the small concerns of the wisteria.

What might a house know?

The chimney blows green bubbles,
uncovers the shape of the cosmos.

The house doesn't like its ears.
It doesn't like to listen to Madonna or Frank Sinatra.

No one ever says *amen* to the speckled wallpaper,

the supporting beam, its creaks and crevices.
Long ago, the house learned to do without

a romantic lover or a lion-clawed tub.
Still, it craves the company of a skogkatt.

If the house could talk it would speak

in cryptograms and Hebrew letters.
It would not propose marriage

to the A-frame next door; paint
itself indigo or wear a little sexy red door

to pass through. Instead, it would nod

goodbye to its foundation,
step out onto the lake, leave the porch light on.

Tonight, I Travel Back to Allston Street

When my father turned nineteen
his father died and no one told him
the truth of dying:

the ocean is for sale today
and you cannot buy it.

In their corner store, *Kosher for Passover*,
labels arrived unaccompanied
by the rabbi's actual prayers

duplicity sticking to each can
of mandarins, each vessel of sour pickles.

The silences could drown a boy,
could slay him
down to a slip of breath—

language drifting between Yiddish and English—
Shabbat candles the only brightness

he could rely on. *Stay bright,
stay bright*, he might have prayed
but probably not.

Perhaps his mind played the periodic tables
or bicycled down tenement avenues.

Here is what he learned:
to perfect invisibility, to become a statue—
an "American" like Buffalo Bill

or the Kennedys. I think of the tides
that grew him—a man with a talent

for happiness and his wife most alive in misery.
The plush and spin of their marriage; green tongues
never watered enough. Angel wing begonias

my father grew in pots of vermiculite—no dirt
allowed in my mother's house, no bugs. What made

him do it? Every year as winter dust tempered
the sun porch he transplanted the starts upstairs
and attic-bound they rested, dormant. Today,

my father, dead 20 years, would be 93. It's hard
to believe it. *Were you his favorite?* my father's best friend

asked as the funeral broke up. And so I took it in
the same way I overheard a student on campus
pleading with his friend, *Do I smell of pancake batter?*

asking as if he really needed to know. So little
it takes to swim beyond the small talk and investigate

the ocean floor. The coral reefs and lost sunglasses,
the obscured treasures of feeling and forms
of intimacy. Only once did my father tell me

I love you. That human line of language, three
syllables and eight letters with two spaces in-between.

It's the in-between where I live now. The
middle of middle age where I paint my house
the blue-grey of Allston Street, to invite back

the person who fathered me, the branched
tributaries in blossom on his birthday, May 20th,
where I will return to him beyond language.

My ghost self and his finally speaking.

First Knowledge

A small room, but it was my room,
in a foreign country on a side street

named after a queen. From my single bed

pushed against sash windows, I listened
to the world of urinating men,

heard hard-accented curse words as bar fights

broke out and couples pushed up against our rooming house
stairs. Upstairs, Ravel's *Bolero* blared

for Leo who believed he'd created the longest orgasm in the world.

When two waitresses appeared
from behind his door, I was not yet

drinking age, uncertain of multiple bodies.

Each morning I'd stare at the mirror—
pour water from a blue pitcher,

then drown in a chipped, porcelain bowl.

A private still-life as the landlady drew
eviction notices for each international boyfriend.

Until I sang *so long*, moving on to document miracles

beyond the sexual, beyond a wall
of makeshift egg cartons: a sound-proofing composition

by the former tenant, a cellist from Senegal.

Elegy for Grace

Tea of conversation over burnt toast
and black currant jam.
Breakfast tea from a pre-warmed cozy,

leaves pressed into the infuser,
offered strong with brown sugar cubes.
Tea of confessions. A shimmering world

of grace, with eggs for breakfast
and a tea pantry of iridescent tins with
luminosity in rows—a gallery exhibit

of Earl Grey; the Prince
of Wales, Darjeeling, Oolong.
Each night another aromatic visitation

as Grace, Paul's mum,
brings her trilogy of thick albums
from the highest bookshelf—

tea-stained photographs of a shy girl
from Liverpool—born between
the wars. Grace of survival.

Grace born of the dockyards
and steel strip mills, whose geologist
son travels to the Himalayas,

to Goa, to Assam. Paul's postcard
arrives from West Bengal: *Teatime!*
A picture of five hundred women

kneeling to pluck leaves, their baskets
filled on the night of summer solstice—
the most lavish tea in the world.

In the English market each Thursday,
cozies and strainers, alchemical objects
unaltered for millennia.

A pinch of leaves left in a teacup:
an acorn, an owl, telling the future
displeased with what it sees.

Tea-flavored mints at the midnight
pharmacy to disguise whisky
or weed at the back of a boy's breath.

The sky, tea-colored, against
poplars and lindens,
mirroring a teapot-shaped pond.

Tea tales so high they tumble
into the next century.
Tea mother who taught infant school

who traveled to class via scooter
commuting along the Calthorpe Close.
Grace of the cigarette

and the tea towel, the late-night
cheese and onion sandwiches.
Grace of the inquisitive mind

imbibing *Midnight's Children*,
in love with the *Life of Pi*.
Tea of generosity.

Grace's wealth measured out in lemon balm,
in well-used spoons. Messages
she writes now on teabag-sized notes:

I am 88 years old. I am grandmother to Rebecca, to Ellie.
Grace featured on the BBC news,
the poster woman for Dementia

and the once-upon-a-time Grace who took me in—
a temporal immigrant/illegal alien—
and became my closest friend, over tea.

Guardian of the Egg

Because not everyone can wear a velvet dress
with a cape of seabirds flying
from her chest towards a hieroglyphic sky,

you stood out—your foul language of hyena
and humpback whale, your omelets
famous for the buttery flavor of red hair.

And in your sketches of a ghost minotaur
with griffin, you conjured an unknown bestiary—
and became yourself.

Nowadays we visit in Seattle—
mornings on the way to work, a shimmer
of angel cake rises from a surreal sky—

you pack my pockets with amulets
in the shapes of clouds and limpet shells.
I am as mysterious to myself as I am to others, you tell me.

In the folded hands of your giantess,
you paint a ginormous egg—kitchen-essential
of beginnings and endings, clairvoyant orb.

The light beams as I guide my ninety-year-old cousin
towards the local YWCA. How she halts, gazing
like a scholar at a mother and infant leaving.

I remember how time unhooked then
as Molly spoke to the newborn:
from one end to the other. And we knew

that the tiny one understood—
how both held edges of the one silk thread—
their own alchemical painting.

Extreme Close-up

All the things I love about his face come from movement:
the fishtail lines, sketched just above the edges
of his cheekbones, a tadpole of a mustache which appears,
then disappears inked along the philtrum—trimmed
to obscure the future. And yes, my father's ears do resemble
oyster shells, sculptures adorned with an outcropping of hair.
Praise be to his widow's peak—un-furrowed and furrowed
like a sail for survival; to his small mouth now open—
ready for a lobster tail or a knish. And somewhere,
perhaps burnishing his jaw or dimpled chin, his father's
early death and the knowledge of his own. I scan the code
in his crescent-shaped eyes. My eyes. DNA spiraling
along a connected shoreline. The taking and giving
back of deep waters; his wonderment hooked to sorrow.

Self Portrait as Leonora Carrington Painting

I never understood how it happened
the doorknob turning left, not right,
until the different selves assembled:
how I recognized myself in the blue chair
like a hangover of sky complete with hyena
and rocking horse. A kind of overworked
alchemy that made the chair legs wear the same
boots that I wore—painted with a delicate dab—
six buttons up the side like soused constellations
working afterhours. And when no one was there,
the horse, shoeless, stumbled out the doorway,
mane matted and unadorned. She
cantered to the orchard for just a moment—
yet, in her clouded loneliness, how she howled—
how she opened her ginger mouth to the sky—
apricots buzzing on the branches as if to join
her. How did she transform from toy
to Pegasus? How do I toss off my blue dress
of missteps and instead choose a star map
that slips me through to another galaxy? Good-bye
to the asparagus of self-doubt, the onionskin envelope
of the lonely. Instead, let this hangover open
into uncharted happiness, let the sweetness be dangerous.
Unfasten the windows from their frames, take off
the rooftop from the triple-decker house—join the hyena,
the horse, and the girl. Offer them wings.

What I Learned from *Bewitched*

A girl could have a boy's name and still be beautiful.
Sometimes exchanges between husband and wife

would be boring—all pot roast and brisket.

Yet, a twitch of the nose and clean dishes
could appear like a universe rewilding—

but what good was traditional magic

if Sam stayed with what's-his-name?
How could anyone love a man

the opposite of handsome, only begrudgingly kind?

What if the network had written her a new lover?
If together, the two women had cleaned the neighborhood

of bigotry, of crime? I watched *Bewitched* as my mother bleached

the kitchen sink, let down hems from hand-me-down coats.
I cast spells and collected international postage stamps—

Abracadabra survival, abracadabra something-something new—

Physics of Causality

I think about bones and fascia, therefore I am
housed in a body; one that has been overstepping itself
lately, like rainwater overflows a pitcher plant.

I think about liberty dimes nested in blue
paper rolls my father kept at the top of his dresser;
therefore, I am still

scaffolded in nostalgia—too little
to reach the lacquered edge—
still awed by its pineapple design.

I think about the physics of causality—
though this might not be a physical thing.
How a hike along a hillside one late summer

evening can later cause a jostle of blood
to flee the uterine lining. A rustling,
and then an outpouring,

through panties and faded jeans
and pillowed living room seats.
I wonder about how the deep plum-

colored story delivered my body
to the 21st century oracle
of sonogram, of biopsy, and then

the reaching up inside to steal
the entire wheelhouse of woman parts.
Therefore, I am awake to recall this,

here in the wake of driftwood and mud,
in turning leaves and woodsmoke on the beach.
I am an organic machine, a light cone—

as Einstein said; here where the whole
calls out its parts: cat fur and fury,
sexual proclivity with mountains, with trees.

Reading the Rising Tides

Most nights along the shoreline, I gaze
at the festival of gulls and gorgeous women,
all with wings and places to go.
My mind moves like a cloudscape
over stippled flashes of blood orange and beach rose.
I read the text of the tides—
the iridescent stones and seaweed,
driftwood and silt.
Against so strong a current you cannot advance.
And yet, we do.
Some days I watch a caftaned
woman playing trumpet to the outgoing waters.
Some nights I meet a man un-digging his coffin
in the sand. Lovers and tough mothers, newborns
with fathers who coo in Creole. We nod briefly—
our pockets overflow with oyster shells
and coins too few for the seaside bar.
What compels us from our houses
even during a pandemic to wonder,
and stroll, and skate.
I look out in wonder
with the others watching
our bright failures, our sea-lit joys.

We Wish to Name It, That's What Humans Do—

In the middle of open waters, wind currents arrive
undocumented like constellations of travelers—

until one wave splits open into the eye of an oleander,
onto the vertebrae of a woman collaging her life back

together in ribbon-cut tiles; her iridescence, consensual
as cloud light. The waves open to an archipelago

of lovers wearing cool outfits in coral, squid ink,
and half shells. Here, you and I can stay up

all night—your Aegean to my Adriatic, my Pacific inlet
to your Atlantic shore. Our floating bridge bodies

tease and cajole, stumble and splash, and rise into one.
Aren't we all made of water? One ocean?

We call love deep or shallow, intricate sexual hieroglyphics
like tide charts or miniature stamps to lick off. Where

shall we send them? In the crested wave, you and I breathe
into blue portals, open to a heartsway called home.

Remedios

In her taxi, the shape of an open blouse,
she plays both passenger and driver,

alchemist and with-it single
woman of the new era.

Where will she travel to—a cigarillo
in one hand, a paintbrush in the other?

Perhaps to a rare archipelago
where seawater tastes of absinthe

and the bushtits offer maps
to lichen temples and jinn-filled

after-hours clubs. A few marriages
later, she arrives as a spirit

level—unbalanced— rising and flying:
a machine of her own creation.

Remedios wears a pair
of rose-flecked wings, suspends them

above her head like an Afghan kite
she conducts by way of strings

slipped in and out of indigo
epilates. Now she's a party

of one searching for late-night cafes
filled with pinball halls and slot machines.

Like the Pythagoreans, she believes
in migrations and math, imagines

the first golf umbrella unearthed under
tablets from the Mesopotamian era.

Later, she'll paint spectral figures
much like herself: archetypal and feral.

Night Windows Above the Street

When she leaves the makeshift curtains
slightly open to the night, her pink slip

slipping slightly above her ruffled ass,

is it her desire to be studied
like a sea anemone or a plum?

Is sight dismantled by the edges of a life,

the scenes we glimpse
or the ones we invent—

stunned into a new realm?

Her body tilts toward a chest
of drawers as if she is in search of a pair of socks

or perhaps she is tending to love.

And if she spied me here
conducting a study of her balcony

and the small bedroom beyond—

most likely she would offer me
her longest finger:

firm, manicured, enameled pink.

A persistent gesture toward the inexplicable—
but I would not look away.

Her yellow radiator whistling

An improbable symphony: *this is
me, this is me.*

Vegetarian vampires walk into a bar

after Remdios Varo

insert straws into fruits and flowers,

drink the lifeblood of a watermelon,
a tomato, a five-petaled rose.

Their faces appear as expressionless

as businessmen
about to go under; their new suits

woven from subsidized chaffs of wheat,

already frayed at the knees.
From underneath twin bowler hats,

flash enormous golden ear wings.

Perhaps they are listening to a botanist's
lament for the dying, or the rap of lemon thyme?

Perhaps we've arrived too late to save the world's

gardens. Still, we will stage protests
in alliance with the waves of grain.

Underneath the vampires' barstools

two pet roosters snore, their combs and wattles
luminous—their speckled collars

hand-carved from the finest melon skins.

You Might Be Wondering Why I Called You Here

Dear ex-lovers, welcome to this floating world
of limbo where break-ups are revisited

and unsentimental critiques offered. Au revoir
to former existences crescendo-ing

over the Olympic Mountains complete with
postcards and maps—affixed

with counterfeit stars. Dear ex-lovers, help
yourself to snacks. I've laid out nuts

with a thought towards metaphor. Stinky cheese
for example. Settle in for some continental

drift of loneliness, time's heartbeat opening
and then closing above the sofa.

Hello Pablo, Ricardo, Saul—
please taste the oysters of angst, the grapes

grown of low self-esteem, the years. God will see you now—
ready with a pen in her hand, a sheaf of parchment.

You are not innominate, your meltdown,
your mistress, your sadness—all here after decades.

You're not my idea of Marilyn Monroe one of you said
on our first and last afternoon together.

That's worth remembering for your death bed.
Limbo is usually for the uncircumcised, the unbaptized

infants who die before their name day, but here you are!
Misunderstood and misaligned you might protest, and I'd agree.

But where are the doorknobs? Where are the doors
that lead out of this cold mind of mine?

Someday I Will Love Susan Rich

Often a woman struggles to mention herself.
She hems and haws like a blackbird,
her gaze turned downwards towards the glitter of a pie
tin or caught by the brass bell hanging from the door
of her dad's corner store. The bird isn't dumb.
It knows that wanting has its own rock bottom
which no tool or stratagem can fix.
Eventually the hawk shows up
in swan's clothing; eventually the garden
fills with chipped mirrors and cracked
dinner plates. But what's wrong with that?
Why not make a collage of wanting?
Isn't it worse not to want? So what
if it ends in disaster? If we finish
in shelter-in-place with only a long pier
of desire, a Legend song
and an evening stroll along the shoreline—
won't it still have been worth it?
I have this idea that I might survive;
find myself brighter than a hummingbird's folly.
Even if I remember none of this;
if the clouds mask the Olympic range
and the air transubstantiates to bread soup—
I am still one superhighway
of flesh and fingertips and kaleidoscopic vision.
Someday, my name and I will enlist
all of ourselves—we'll sign on for a lifetime
membership to exist in a seal call, inhabit
one incisor of a cascade fox.

True Story

I lived in a coat closet, a stone garden, a sweater of English wool.
I lived with a would-be murderer, a pickpocket, a woman
who closely resembled a kangaroo.

I lived on the shoreline of a desert, in a nation of bells,
a saltbox. I lived on a tune.

And I traveled by taxicab, by camel back,
led astray by a hurly-burly heart, a lifetime of overtime,
of *fly away* and *thank you.*

I waited in abeyance for the map of my life
to unfold. For the tea mug to turn into gold, for the local abbess

to declare we're found, we're saved, we're already here—
on our way to heaven with blue tissue paper
and a carton of wild pears.

A 99-Year-Old Woman Wakes to Find

In the morning she finds it—
a kinkajou curled on her chest

like an unexamined question.

Its tail loops around her waist
and the stubs of the ears twitch—

the thick snout wet against her neck.

The woman murmurs in half sleep,
keeps calm (her husband gone some decades).

And now this living warmth—

the open window, the clock's hands,
the glass of water by the bed—

shimmer as she strokes

its matted fur, feels the breathing
of this feral thing she's never known before—

and is not frightened by the scent

of pungent dirt and piss.
In her mind a green canopy reopens

of breadfruit and palms

overhung with hummingbirds
and Juan's contralto song.

She moves her lips along his beard,

follows through the deep heart's core—
ecstatic in this dual citizenship.

Tired of Being a Woman

As it happens, I am tired of being a woman.
Exhausted by the bathroom scale,
the carnal ins and outs,
of who did what to whom.
I am tired of rosehip serums

that the persistent cats lick off.
Tired of chamomile facemasks—
my forehead iridescent
as a lacquered carousel horse.
I am tired of my country.

Tired of my feet, of searching for husbands
like commuters claim their train cars:
one, in a dark and empty space,
another, a little off the rails.
Instead, I'd prefer to be a corner store

with an echoing bell of *welcome*.
The attainable pleasures—chocolate bars,
honeyed challah, yellow tulips in winter.
Honestly, I am exhausted from walking
home alone past kneeling lovers, past swans.

I don't want to go on paddling
towards fascism in the West; I don't want
another pizza or to watch the fallen
B stars on New Year's Eve.
I can't go on as a pair of eyeglasses.

I cruise the local ice cream parlors, the salons,
the table-linen restaurants that thrust the scent of sirloin
and rum onto the sidewalk; that scarf-up the
mortgage payment, the safety net, the lifetime
of save and save and save. All I want

is the frisson that comes from an operatic sky,
from another stroll at dusk. All I want: my lover's
lips on the lower curve of my back. I want
the shoreline where sea lions appear and almost
wave to me as they warm their flippers in the briny air.

Self Portrait with Stained Glass and Feathers

As she works, everything wakes-up
and takes notice: from the alembic

paint-machine assistant, to the magnifying
glass that she uses to render tropical

birds—Merlins and Yucatan Nightjars—
that soon exit her canvas, then spiral above

the church windows into a ghost
night, over-poured with bright constellations

which the painter lightens into breathing orbs;
the same shape that her brown, raptor-like face

takes as she concentrates on her vision—
and though the birds exhaust her, she pulls

each one out from her musical heart:
the perfect body part for a woman transitioning

to an owl—which every girl knows—
will require more than a prayer and a spell.

We Are All God's Poems

In the beginning, no one did their assigned tasks.
When God was supposed to create different genders

they found themselves staring into an inland waterway
wondering how many droplets could slide over a stone

in a moment. God was like that, she lived for riddles.
She'd calculate a finite number of compounds, hydrogen

copycatting twerk moves and oxygen two-stepping up-close.
Who knew water could be so malleable? Neither male nor female—

without color, or, more honestly, infinite colors iridescing.
No one asked water if it came from a rib; did it know a certain serpent?

God kept opalescent eyes on the covalent bonds, deconstructing
the anatomy of water which seemed a slippery notion at best,

like the idea of designing and drywalling the world in seven days.
Who would believe it! God hummed a little as molecules

kept growing and so did all genders, their hair like waterfalls.
Somewhere God read a billion seconds would take 32 years to count...

They napped then; stretched their neck like a house cat
or perhaps a Tyrannosaurus Rex. And what about cloud genders?

A bank, a billow, a scape? How much water might God transition in
via communal faucet, lake effect, favorite swimming hole?

How to Travel in the Middle Period

Say *yes!* to the open-scabbed dog
that accompanies you
through the village—

and *yes!* to the wood ash—
that rises-up daily
from the workers' rooms—

to the farmer on his tractor
who from across a broad
distance calls to you,

bonjour, madame, ça va?
on your first Atlas Mountain
morning in Oumass.

Say *oui!* to the tribe of cats
and wood turtles that appear along
the lip of the pool

waiting for a bite of the sunbathers
bananas. Taste *yes!*
in the breakfast of argan butter

and almonds; tattoo *yes!*
to the remaining you and
the changing you—

to the first full-body scrub.
Watch as parts of you roll
and scatter as the Moroccan

woman leads you from the steam hall,
to shower, to bath (*yes!*)
anointed with oils of geranium and rose.

And so you've learned to travel
through multiple waters and sky—
in the glide and drift of it—

like tree goats that forage,
then build their lives mid-air—
knowing *yes!* as the one chosen thing.

from

THE CARTOGRAPHER'S TONGUE
(2000)

The Mapparium

Boston, Massachusetts

In geography class we learn the world
of oceans, continents, and poles. We race
our fingers over mountain ranges and touch
rivers lightly with felt-tip markers. Deserts, islands,
and peninsulas tumble raw and awkward
off our tongues. *Kalahari, Sumatra, Arabia.*

We visit the Mapparium on a field trip.
A made-up word we learn
for the place where the world resides.
We clamor in with falling socks and high-octave squeals
Palermo, Kabul, Shanghai,
exploring the globe, crossing its circumference we take flight—
touch down on the see-through bridge.

The earth as it was, a time called 1932,
stays in a room—retracts our breath,
our lives—makes history into color and light.
We look up at the Baltics, see *Lithuania, Latvia, Estonia,*
lands my grandmother left. Sixteen
and wanting the world.

I want to stay inside this world, memorize
the pattern of blue that reveals
the origins of every sea.
A wave hitting stone is the sound my voice leaves
as a pledge to return on the glass.
Feet to Antarctica, arms outstretched
like beacons towards Brazil—
I'll take this globe as my own.

Nomadic Life

Republic of Niger

When I come back with the cups of tea
the sugar bowl has been emptied,
my imported M&M's—
gone. Flies stretch their legs
search, then spiral
in a dust storm of light.
Aisha sits solemn in afternoon heat
examines the inside of ice cubes
questions what makes water
strong or weak.
We invent common words between us,
point at the refrigerator door,
the photograph of ferns rising out of snow
the last volunteer left behind.
I'd like to trade with her
my typewriter keys
for the way she navigates the desert
reads the coordinates of sand.
I want to know as Aisha knows
when it's time to follow
the ambivalent line of landscape
keep faith in dunes that disappear.
By evening when she tastes
my color-coated chocolates,
shares them with her friends—
we both will recall the nomad
the other woman
we each might have been.

Lost by Way of Tchin-Tabarden

Republic of Niger

Nomads are said to know their way by an exact spot in the sky,
the touch of sand to their fingers, granules on the tongue.

But sometimes a system breaks down. I witness a shift of light,
study the irregular shadings of dunes. Why am I traveling

this road to Zinder, where really there is no road? No service station
at this check point, just one *commerçant* hawking *Fanta*

in gangrene hues. *C'est formidable!* he gestures—staring ahead
over a pyramid of foreign orange juice.

In the desert life is distilled to an angle of wind, camel droppings,
salted food. How long has this man been here, how long

can I stay contemplating a route home?
It's so easy to get lost and disappear, die of thirst and longing

as the Sultan's three wives did last year. Found in their Mercedes,
the chauffeur at the wheel, how did they fail to return home

to Ágadez, retrace a landscape they'd always believed?
No cross-streets, no broken yellow lines; I feel relief at the abandonment

of my own geography. I know there's no surveyor but want to imagine
the aerial map that will send me above flame trees, snaking

through knots of basalt. I'll mark the exact site for a lean-to
where the wind and dust travel easily along my skin,

and I'm no longer satiated by the scent of gasoline. I'll arrive there
out of balance, untaught; ready for something called home.

Lessons in the Desert

for Sa-a

The Wodaabe aren't allowed to read
or write their names
in spiral-bound notebooks
as I taught the boy to do.
After allowing our visits for months,
friendship propagating like a stubborn weed,
they accepted his forays into the peculiar,
the way of life inside my home.

How he played the music
imprisoned in a silver box,
stood in streams of water
falling from a ceiling pipe,
and shared peanut sauce spread on bread
instead of as he was used to.

But it was this word he'd learned to write,
the name which meant the lucky one,
Sa-a, that made them whip the bridge
of his nose, the lashes and soft lids
as if to keep his eyes shut tight,

closed against schools of any sort—
and other things nomads had no use for.
Survival meant to keep him
from slipping away,
from getting lost in the lines of the page.

The Filigree of the Familiar

Gaza City, Gaza

Here, all the men wear mustaches
which decorate their faces
in soft curved designs.
Mornings they bring me tangerines,
faux French bread,
and the daily day-old news.

The mustaches shift in color, shape, and size
depending on the wishes of each man
to expose his better self; to project his own
combed landscape: a miniature scissors,
a mirror in his hand.
So many mustaches! Such strange lands!
Some thick as kitchen brooms,
smooth as the Negev sands; Ibrahim's
opaque as winter light
brushed from the rim of the moon.

In laundry rooms, in stairwells,
in cities, on continents, there are periscopes
and clocks, garbage cans and front door lights
that whisper shyly if we just stand still
a warrantee will be provided
with instructions for our lives:
how to settle for less, how not to grow old.

Do I leave to take a stand?
Or circle around the globe,
passport in-hand to get away from the incessant
no-win scenes, the frantic filigree of the familiar
pressing like dead dreams inside my head?

And is it right that I speak of the women of Gaza
in their hijabs and long sleeves,
to imagine stories of their domestic breathing?
Must I turn away from Ramallah, Hebron,

the East Gate entry way? Decline sweet offers
from Yusef and Samir—
not dance at Omar's wedding
but keep my body alone?

But then, if I describe only what is already inscribed,
I'd never see the black man on my street
who sweeps with an imaginary broom,
never see the Indian Ocean
assert itself, then recede.

We move about the world
watching for signs of what we already know
is best; a parenthesis of photographs to pause in,
an isolated palm lined beach to rest.
And at what point do I become the souvenir?
A faceless history set in amber?

Must I write only of hometown corners
swan boats, street cars, Boston Harbor—
to stay in the odd intersections
New Englanders call Squares?
And which house is the home where I remain?
Juggler Meadow Road or Edinburgh?
Devon Street or Chelsea?
Home or travel, and which is which
and whose choice is it to say?

And if home might be any dot on the map—
maybe the one which is furthest away,
then I'll find mine only with a telescope.
Somewhere there's a life with tethered satellite
linking the outbound voyage to the everyday.

The Wall

What superstition and fanaticism on every side.

THEODORE HERZL

We Jews slip secrets inside cracked mortar
the flap of an envelope
half a postcard from home.

Call them prayers or wishes,
reasons why one must travel continents
to ask in person
for advice or apology.

Here is the mailbox of God
where a woman walks backwards
after praying, never turning
her back to the wall.

Above her head tiny airplanes
originate explosions
scuttle across orchid blue sky
intent on their military exercise.

A hard light binds weathered stone
bleaches the guard-studded square
where a neighborhood was razed in a night.
Mosques and homes. Mosques and homes.

Whatever Happened to the Bodies...

I listen to my radio not for music, but the news.
The Orthodox are out again behind the yellow lines,
They're scraping blood off sidewalks, limbs from city streets.

Whatever happened to the skin of memory?
Whatever happened to the elbows, kneecaps, teeth?
Whatever passes for tenderness only veils our disbelief.

I listen to Linda Gradstein as I *Comet* clean the kitchen sink.
Every scrap of flesh, every drop of blood, you try to get it, she repeats.
Behind my house the raku kiln is firing masks and beads.

Whatever happened to the bodies cut and maimed?
Whatever held the hand which lit the gas?
Whatever scenario we imagine, we miscast.

I listen ready to participate—scrubbing souls from Tel Aviv's streets.
Propel the senses to migrate beyond what I can think.
The prayers I'm meant to remember, the unutterable, the indistinct.

Whatever happened to the bodies without names?
Whatever became of people cannibalized, drowned, depraved?
Whatever moves us eventually moves away.

I listen to the neighbors in their yard:
Angel, Silver, Red, and Ma. I move
with concentrated ease, dusk is smothering the trees.

Whatever happens to the bodies still alive?
Whatever exuberance may they hold?
Whatever dies returns to us to be retold.

The Palmist

She touches a stranger's hand, turns it into the light.
Examines the spacing of fingers, the arc of his thumb,
the way the headline forks towards Upper Mars.
She takes in the whole from the curve of his wrist
to the pink inside the nails. She learns the language of his hand.

She measures flexibility, admires the sculpture of knuckles,
the relationship of flesh to bones. In the islands, branches, stars
meaning unfolds. Words she cannot anticipate
come from her lips. She knows more than she tells.

Every hand she reads is a map she gets to travel,
a master plan of past with potential lives.
She touches the mounts, then fingers the chains—
uncovers another's journey and holds on.

She knows the Kabbalah of the Jews, the Brahmin's Hindu Vedas.
She knows nothing is written until we write it
and rewrite it again, that it's desire that alters destiny
that all of our lines will change.

Ghazal for the Woman from Vitez

Vitez, Bosnia Herzegovina

It's the best watermelon in the world
but there's no way to say it in words.

She had squatted in the space for apples and pears
under the staircase, one year, beyond the place of words.

Now she comes back with tea, examines me closely,
my out-of-date phrase book, my mispronounced words.

I ask for the toilet and she shows me the bedrooms, bombed
by neighbors who should have known how to use words.

We walk out to her garden in late afternoon light,
survey squash plants and cornstalks, we re-enter words.

In Bosnian the tomato is called *paradise*, sweetness
transferred from some other country's words.

We drink rounds of whisky, call her sons on the phone
laughing because we have found a way out through words.

Wendy

Wendy, Wendy when you are sleeping in your silly bed
you might be flying about with me saying funny things to the stars.
"Wendy," he said, "how we should all respect you."

Peter Pan

This time she would know better.
There would be no sewing shadows
mending the boys' tails, hot afternoons
cooking alligator, skinning
the pirates for stew.
She'd rather walk the plank.
Why would she go with him?
After the storytelling
windows open to the night
she would not be fooled by promises
of fairy dust or tempted with the offer
of mothering lost boys.
No patience with false Romance
she'd go only for the flying—
a movement like magnets to the stars.
Second to the right
and straight on till morning.
Air travel would win her over.
Energized, she'd start a union
for the mermaids
find counseling for Peter
and be off again.
She'd move above volcanoes, investigate
a tangle of clouds.
And then like the pilot resisting
the runway home, she'd hold her breath
and offer up this
pleasure—the telling
of the journey out alone.

Lines Written Before Seeing an Ex-Lover
Who Has Become a Sex Therapist
Instead of a Mathematician

She's curious what advice
he gives his clients
whether she should request
a consultant's fee

for teaching him to knead
her neck and shoulders,
for leading guided walks
underneath her breasts, her hips, her chin.

What do you say to an ex-lover
now specializing
in cajoling sweet fevers
from other peoples' limbs—

pass the butter please,
how do you like your fish?
Dinner conversation may drift
to a lexicon of innuendo

or surprise, a marlin filet
mistaken for a shirt
of crêpe de Chine.
Will she let herself

evoke their first seduction
over strawberries and tea,
his summer-colored body
eager for the lessons

she promised
in advanced geometry?
They'll postulate theorems
in concentric circles,

polygons, and trapezoids,
coordinate arcs
and draw right angles
along perpendicular,

and then parallel sides.
Does he ever use her
as a textbook illustration
of *unproven symmetry?*

Or in stressing sexual
misconduct among tutors of the *GRE?*
He'll check his watch, apologize,
an appointment he must keep.

But in the garage, they'll linger
by rectangles of *Honda, Camaro, Jeep.*
And when they finally kiss
his mouth urgent and deep,

she'll greet the radius of his tongue,
finger the slope of his thigh. And wiser now,
she'll keep to her belief in independent lines;
and mouth the words *good night.*

Love in the Time of AIDS

You are afraid
of a moist toothbrush, disposable razor,
fearful of the inside
of your lover's mouth.
Too terrified to pose an inquiry in shorthand
positive, negative?
You imagine your date's response
I don't know.
Remembering the scent of one man
the fingertips of another
triggers the inevitable moment
when your eyes
search this new body, stop
and check for signs—
like a pilot before the flight
records temperature and distance
knowing even this cannot ensure a safe journey.

The lovers he's had before
are now your lovers
and yours are his
their health and habits as migratory
as your own blood.

In the morning
you telephone for the test
anonymously. No way to study or plan.
The voice at the end of the line
gives you the number you will use
as your identity, sets a time and place
where you meet a man named Manuel.
No hint of this, no mark
will mar your records.

You bargain with yourself.
You'll give up kissing—
no more dancing
of tongues. You promise to become
a condom connoisseur. Take six-month tests
for HIV as if they were multiple choice.
As if the pilot knows whether or not the plane
will crash or glide across the sky,
as if the sky knows what is written underneath its skin.

Haiti

It's 4 a.m. on her birthday
as she prepares for morning mass
wanting the luck
early prayers are said to bring.

Today she's turning sixteen
and the only one awake.
She brushes her hair back, drawing
it into a braid, puts in the silver earrings
tiny as insect eyes, and turns to admire
the curve of her legs in silk stockings.

She spies her brother's jacket
lifts it from the hook, singing under her breath.
The day is fine. The breeze feels cool along
the edge of her skin. She walks out on to the porch.
A shadow blocks her way down the stairs,
a body propped against bougainvillea
rigid against clay pots.

Here is a gift from the TonTon Macoute,
someone's brought Papa home.
A note pinned to his collar like a caption
she writes for her scrapbook. The face is
swollen, the soles of the feet burnt,
the lips one long purple bruise.
This family has 24 hours to leave.

There are no words to remember,
no beginning or end to this day.
Her mother puts them on the boat,
nodding good-bye from the dock,
I will join you.
The girl wonders when they became flecks
of glass, bits of color thrown out to sea.

She listens to the priest bless their voyage,
wondering at the words *asylum seekers*, doesn't know
she is one of ten thousand faces, that those like her
are not believed, are sent home, followed, and will leave

again. She watches her mother turn into the horizon.

Oslobođenje

The first year of the siege
we changed sizes thirteen times,

no one expected to see
a paper come out of those flames.

Yes, we had losses.

The local correspondent in Zvornick,
our finance clerk traveling between offices.

Yet, on that last bus out of the city,
no one wanted to leave.

The paper migrated from yellow to blue to green.

There was just bread and paper,
and there were many days without bread.

Bosnia and Herzegovina

Muted Gold

My father died just as my plane touched down.
He taught me journeys don't happen in straight lines.
I loved him without ever needing words.
Is memory a chain of alibis?

He taught me journeys don't happen in straight lines.
His father sailed Odessa to Boston Harbor.
Is memory a chain of alibis?
The story I choose a net of my own desires?

His father sailed Odessa to Boston Harbor.
Dad worked beside him in their corner store.
The story I choose a net of my own desires?
I wish I'd known to ask the simple questions.

Dad worked beside him in their corner store.
They shelved the tins of black beans, fruit preserves, and almond cakes.
I wish I'd known to ask the simple questions,
he'd have stayed with me and gossiped over toast.

They shelved the tins of black beans, fruit preserves and almond cakes.
What colors did they wear, what languages were spoken?
He'd have stayed with me and gossiped over toast,
now he's smiling but I can't summon the thoughts he's thinking.

What colors did they wear, what languages were spoken?
Was it a muted gold, a world of shattered feeling?
Now he's smiling but I can't summon the thoughts he's thinking.
I pack his clothes away, mark them *for Goodwill.*

Was it a muted gold, a world of shattered feeling?
What good will it do to dwell, I hear him say.
I pack his clothes away, mark them for *Goodwill.*
but I hold fast to one old T shirt, butter-smooth, and brilliant.

What good will it do to dwell, I hear him say.
He much preferred to glide along life's surface.
But I hold fast to one old T shirt, butter-smooth, and brilliant
and tell a story by moonlight, to try and keep him with me.

He much preferred to glide along life's surface.
I love him now with images, with words,
and tell a story by moonlight, to try and keep him with me.
My father died just as my plane touched down.

from

CURES INCLUDE TRAVEL
(2006)

What She Leaves Unspoken

When she is blue she is not kingfisher,
jacaranda, yew.

She is not a river tide

or drum roll; not a periwinkle
bolt of fabric,

a French matchstick
gone unused, but the grime on

beveled glass, the battered cup, the small

hole in your left shoe. She cannot move
one dormant arm above

the hydrangea of her mind—

no kitchen clock, no metronome
measures this conscripted time, this Tuareg scarf of blue.

She is a knot, a ridge, an open wound,

a clue without an answer. No country
tune, no catalogue of saints

can bring her out, across the way.

No, she is not air, nor unstitched wrist,
nor Mary's Bosnian brood;

when she is blue, she is not you
but an absent text, an unreliable X.

Mohamud at the Mosque

for my student upon his graduation

And some time later in the lingering
blaze of summer, in the first days
after September 11th you phoned—

*if I don't tell anyone my name, I'll
pass for an African American.*
And suddenly, this seemed a sensible solution—

the best protection: to be a black man
born in America, more invisible than
Somali, Muslim, asylum seeker—

Others stayed away that first Friday
but your uncle insisted that you pray.
How fortunes change so swiftly,

I hear you say. And as you parallel
park across from the Tukwila
mosque, a young woman cries out—

her fears unfurling beside your battered car
go back where you came from!
You stand, both of you, dazzling there

in the mid-day light, her pavement
facing off along your parking strip.
You tell me she is only trying

to protect her lawn, her trees,
her untended heart—already
alarmed by its directive.

And when the neighborhood
policeman appears, asks
you, asks her, asks all the others—

So what seems to be the problem?
He actually expects an answer,
as if any of us could name it—

as if perhaps your prayers
chanted as this cop stands guard
watching over your windshield

during the entire service
might hold back the world
we did not want to know.

Annaghmakerrig, 4 a.m.

County Monaghan

The later the hour, the more convinced
I become of voices outside
$\qquad\qquad\qquad$ traveling
through the courtyard, the conservatory;

opulent bass tones of men
$\qquad$ paired with a woman's brighter laughter.

$\qquad\qquad\quad$ Up along the tree canopy
the phrases linger .

$\qquad$ reassembling into light

$\qquad\qquad\qquad$ branches of matter.

Sounds rustling each to each:
$\qquad$ Russian cheers, a Siberian drumbeat.

(They must be soaked to the bone by now.)

In the tea kettle's mist one small shout—
$\qquad\qquad\qquad$ the timbre closer

$\qquad$ then further away

across to the other side of the lake.
Before morning comes,

$\qquad\qquad\qquad$ before I brave the blue
shore and touch the sun

I listen again to the torn cloth of music.

A Poem for Mr. Raphael Siv
at the Irish Jewish Museum

Portobello, Dublin 8

Write a poem for the museum you demanded
as if you could order a poem the way you
order a bagel, toasted or with lox and cream cheese.

Or even one line. And this second plea
is what persuades me that you, Mr. Raphael Siv,
are a man who believes in poetry.

And why not? Aren't you Irish *and* Jewish?
a heritage any writer would covet, hurriedly
convert to, if it were that easy.

And yet, clearly this vigil of yours sparks its own
kind of artistry. When you set off to work
each morning, traveling down the South Circular

Road, can you sense the museum's
awakening beyond its curtains, prayer
shawls, and scrolls? As you open the interior

doors to the former Walworth Synagogue,
I imagine you welcomed in by the Shekinah,
your own bright *avodah*. Upstairs, the bride and

groom will greet you and the pews with the brass
plaques removed will recite their humble blessing
for their *zaddik*, their storyteller, for you.

The Dead Eat Blueberry Scones for Breakfast

with a touch of butter and sweet cream,
a cup of black coffee to reenact the morning;

some food, some drink, soon opens
awakening to a new place. One swan

keening as she circles our silvered lake.

The dead skim the headlines of the *Irish Times*,
re-imagine the aroma of eggs on toast;

they mime the domesticity we simply
breathe in and then just as recklessly let go—

our every action alive with their echo.

They're hovering over our shoulders
as we buy blood oranges

off the back of the young man's truck;
wave good-bye as he leaves

so suddenly. This evening the dead keep singing,

She is the belle of Belfast City,
then finger the jug of red wine

lingering near a woman's arms
alive in this careless air.

Photograph, May 10, 1933

Where one burns books, one will in the end burn people.

Heinrich Heine

At twenty-one, she is tired of learning
the subjunctive, assimilating the facts

inside her brain: cartography, the Ottomans,
the glory of Europe's trains.

So a torchlight parade, bonfires by the opera house
sounded fine when her brother urged,

Come on. She conjured human voices,
smoke-filled cars, the pepper scent of men—

felt ready for conquest, to question the faith of angels;
ready for anything—anything but

an old manure cart dragged up
and down the library steps; Helen Keller

evicted along with Einstein, then Marx.
The orchestra collaborating

with the crowd, the familiar call
of classmates now locked in a medieval scene

and her brother joining in.
And so it begins on a pyre of light—

words spark but the girl averts her eyes
unstoppable   inconceivable   pain.

Everyone in Bosnia Loves Begonias

On balconies safer than passport pages

bright, hard blossoms light up
bullet-worn apartments. Amidst the cracks

from mortar shells—begonias—

Rex Begonias: the commonly-
grown, taken-for-granted,

impossible-to-kill—
flowers are flourishing.

They work in the dirt.

While no one else in Europe
or America interferes,

like a strong neighbor,
the Rex Begonia is there—

in packs and tribes in Travnik,
Banja Luka, Prijedor,

guarding porch doors with serrated leaves—
preserving each family's story.

The Serbian soldier never imagined

the carbon dioxide source
that ricocheted his hand grenade

off the garden window. Across intermediary
boundary lines, strong-stemmed survivors

testify. The begonia has come a long way.
These partisans deflect all praise

for horticultural acts they've staged
and as it is with taxi drivers,

and cigarette vendors,
everyone in Bosnia adores begonias.

Bright light, no light—it's all the same to them:
budding begonias bursting

through the night.

Change

He doesn't register me
as anything more or less
unique than the flawed light

the streetlamp feeds to the hibiscus
tree that watches the corner
café of this empty street.

We collect here most evenings,
late, as if arranged, as if
we might share a scrap of

language and appear
legitimate as lovers:
for any passerby to see—

one body leaning
toward another—fingertips
meeting; *the figures blurred,*

an onlooker might say,
an odd pairing. How much
easier it is to acquiesce

to the alchemist's nation:
a new constitution, a policy,
findings of Truth and Reconciliation.

But this man right here
untethered from the ordinary,
still insists on his interior

gaze, his fraying chord
of grace. This man who nests
underneath the café eaves

tonight looks up and almost
nods to me—to me, not the stranger
from a distant country.

As he murmurs to himself
an indecipherable
blessing, I touch his

palms, pouring my change
into his two cupped
and gorgeous hands.

Fissure

Around midnight, I'm driving
after losing my home, my now

ex-fiancé's words to me,
I can do better echoing

like the quick trill of car alarms,
fever-pitched, three parts forlorn.

And while I'm waiting for the light
to move away from red,

away from my body
traveling alone,

the door locks down—

I notice the cramped shoulders,
the skin caked in white

grime and street dust, a boy's
body, legs outstretched,

sitting on a roundabout
in the middle of the night, in Cape Town.

Barefoot, broadfaced, alone—
I've passed by him before, caught

in my lover's gaze, in jazz
riffs or the daily day-old news.

And perhaps this blindness
can't be contained, but in this city

where children grow plentiful
as pomegranate seeds

on traffic islands, street corners, outside

the parking lot of every apartment
block—and this is harder

to admit, that our thirst rises
beyond response, beyond

what it seems any one of us could
reconcile, could believe:

the flint and fissure of our
time's brutality.

And this is why, the child gives up
on begging for the night,

to take this roundabout
as his own; this unsheltered,

unremarkable, useless in a storm
cement circle with piecrust of stone—

because this is simply where the faltering world
can for one night remain contained;

here—where we all speak like beggars
with little precaution for the rain.

The Men You Don't Get to Sleep With

Are always the men that you want;
the ones who hide something

in their long-fingered hands
and won't let you touch it or tap it;

who refuse your good offerings
of dark chocolate and flan;

the men who come quoting
Keats, who winter in Cannes,

who summit Rainier
without ropes or brains.

These fleeting men; fantasies
we hold for years past their time,

one lone kiss from a cabinetmaker,
all-night laughter with a Bosnian

jailer, the amaranth flavor
of a passionate painter. No,

that's not it, it's not what you think.
Not needing that junk but the act

of his tongue licking crumbs,
soft breath in your ear as he offers,

This is actually fun.
Caleb, Dan, the photographer man;

the ones with crushed hearts
and the ones who had none.

Damn these men, remembered
unnaturally long; did their bodies

shelter something lacquered and spun,
something even today, you wish that

you'd won? But what if sexual
climax was reached with the barista,

the sculptor, the sheik? What then?
Then what would we do?

The riddle undressed, the pleasure
no more than ho-hum.

Better to keep imagining this:
an allusive rhyme, enhanced and revised

on mountain paths, window seats,
private jets, the men that you don't get

you do get: set in pen and ink,
fantasy and less grief—

they can unceasingly please.

A Poem for Will, Baking

He stands before
the kitchen island, begins again
from scratch: chocolate, cinnamon, nutmeg;
he beats, he folds, keeps faith
in what happens
when you combine known quantities,
bake twelve minutes at a certain heat.
The other rabbis, the scholars,
teenagers idling by the beach,
they receive his offerings,
in the early hours, share his grief.
It's enough now, they say.
Each day more baked goods to friends,
and friends of friends, even
the neighborhood dogs. He can't stop,
holds on to the rhythmic opening
and closing of the oven,
the timer's expectant ring.
I was just baking, he says if
someone comes by. Again, and again,
evenings winter into spring,
he creates the most fragile
of confections: madeleines
and pinwheels, pomegranate crisps
and blue florentines;
each crumb to reincarnate
a woman—a savoring
of what the living once could bring.

The Women of Kismayo

The breasts of Kismayo assembled
along the mid-day market street.

No airbrushed mangoes, no
black lace, no underwire chemise.

No half-cupped pleasures,
no come-hither nods, no Italian

centerfolds. Simply the women
of the town telling their men

to take action, to do something
equally bold. And the husbands

on their way home, expecting
sweet yams and meat,

moaned and covered their eyes,
screamed like spoiled children

dredged abruptly from sleep—
incredulous that their women

could unbutton such beauty
for other clans, who

(in between splayed
hands) watched quite willingly.

*Give us your guns, here is our
cutlery, we are the men!*

the women sang to them
an articulation without shame.

And now in the late-night hour
when the men want nothing but rest,

they fold their broken bodies, still
watched by their wives' cool breasts

round, full, commanding as colonels—
two taut nipples targeting each man.

Kismayo, Somalia

Not a Prayer

Now with late afternoon light
rising off the floorboards and

gold-washed window frames,
a hushed air of attentiveness

massages walls to yellow streams.

The table in the vestibule,
oak chair, and lavender

blue bowl, show themselves to be
honey, butter, mustard seed.

And I take what is shimmering
into my body

stand still, living still, for the first time all day.

I wait for the sunlight to speak,
to remind me how

transformation happens
regularly as dusk enraptures day—

the half-averted gaze, the glass,
the morphine placed by her bedside.

Flight Path

On the ascent I let go—

let my life drift
        to the side like litter.

In the complicity of wings
        I tend towards naming

freeway, river, mountain town—
        reaching beyond a horizon

where everything is travel, everything
        enlivened along its open path.

You ask if I'm lonely—

Is there a word for laundry
        dried in moonlight?

A name for the night cries
        of couples in early spring?

And if I could cajole the physical
        into deep belief,

if a drop of honey on the tongue,
        could be *learning*, or say, *love.*

You ask why I go—

to where imagination holds
        the small blue craft of conversation,

to a life of evening song
        lived between the white spaces of now, of gone;

to come to pleasures of the heart, in the mouth,
    when the tongue conducts

Star Thistle, Warbler, Petroglyph.

Listen, what if we could leave here—

with more than velocity, more
    than a thump, then a moan, could we

grasp the silver glint of sandpipers
    as they angle from water to air,

their bodies arced in unison
    hesitant, illumed, bare—

At the Corner of Washington and Third

You could start your life over, sitting here
believe only in roses,

blue oleander, an orange lily.

Clean white table with rocking chair
would be enough.

Early morning, now—

the self returns to the self.

One pear scone, decanter of tea—
and the world appears terribly healthy.

In the rise of river light

open palms of poplar trees
barn swallows state swallow beliefs.

No terrorist in sight.

To the right of the fishpond
the cat claims a gray stone for her own.

The hardest thing of all

would be to choose
your own life.

from

THE ALCHEMIST'S KITCHEN
(2010)

Different Places to Pray

Everywhere, everywhere she wrote; something is falling—
a ring of keys slips out of her pocket into the ravine below;

nickels and dimes and to do lists; duck feathers from a gold pillow.
Everywhere someone is losing a favorite sock or a clock stops

circling the day; everywhere she goes she follows the ghost of her
heart; jettisons everything but the shepherd moon, the hopeless cause.

This is the way a life unfolds: decoding messages from profiteroles,
the weight of mature plums in late autumn. She'd prefer a compass

rose, a star chart, text support messages delivered from the net,
even the local pet shop—as long as some god rolls away the gloss

and grime of our gutted days, our global positioning crimes.
Tell me, where do you go to pray—a river valley, a pastry tray?

Tulip Sutra

The letters that make up "lale," the Turkish word for "tulip,"
are the same as those that form Allah."

—from *Tulipomania*

Praise the origin
of the frilled double latte:

lofty wildflowers on a rocky ledge.

Praise tulips from Turkey,
tulips from China,

tulips born in Afghanistan—

      *

Praise the turbulence
of desire tucked inside

this hobo flower

glimpsed along highways—
small pink vases—

transforming evenings
into reckless weekends.

      *

Before the flowers
depart the harbor, bless

one Istanbul merchant

as he scatters his gift
into bolts of bottle-blue cloth—

praise this small token:

tulips for a foreign friend.

*

And the Flemish merchant
who opens the crates

mistakes the bulbs for coarse, funny onions

seasons them
in vinegar-mint—

but keeps a handful back for his garden—

remember him.

*

How not to believe
in a flower which honors lips

in its names:

Increaser of Pleasure,
Rose of the Dawn,
My Light of Paradise.

Bless each blossom that opens and opens

traveling beyond itself

as it flutters, disheveled
by the bedroom door.

*

Dutch tulips succeeded
in breeding

with tulips coming
from Crete, from Kurdistan;

this intermingling is key

to the Netherlands historical
oligarchy.

*

In spring, bless the farmers of Skagit,
who plant acre upon acre

the tractors, the hands
that nurture each offset

until the lyric flares—

into tulips of feather, of flame.

*

And yes to a tapestry
shielding man from misfortune

more precious than song or sword;

the Sultan's son saved—
by a constellation of tulips

embroidered into his underclothes.

Bless the thread that connects
us to him.

*

Praise the curious tourist
appearing late April

despite winds, and rain, and muck—

who finds her way
by the edge of lit fields—

to witness in one
collusion of color

the return of tulips in flight—

the morning sky
upstaged by a blaze of delight.

Food for Fallen Angels

If food be the music of love, play on—

Twelfth Night, misremembered

If they can remember living at all, it is the food they miss:
a plate of goji berries, pickled ginger, gorgonzola prawns
dressed on a bed of miniature thyme, a spoon

glistening with pomegranate seeds, Russian black bread
lavished with July cherries so sweet, it was dangerous to revive—
to slide slowly above the lips, flick and swallow—almost, but not quite.

Perhaps more like this summer night: lobsters in the lemon grove
a picnicker's trick of moonlight and platters; the table dressed
in gold-kissed glass, napkins spread smooth as dark chocolate.

If they sample a pastry—glazed Florentine, praline hearts—
heaven is lost. It's the cinnamon and salt our souls return for—
rocket on the tongue, the clove of garlic: fresh and flirtatious.

At Middle Life: A Romance

Let love be imminent and let it be a train;
let it arrive at dawn, its whistle whiskering the air—

all brightness and verb. Let it nearly race by
but not quite— this could be the rhythm of your life.

Don't hesitate outside the dining car of eccentric
and dark-eyed strangers, conjuring their espresso—

ordering half the nerve. Let love be a breakfast
of crème cakes, pomegranate juice, a lively Spanish tortilla.

Love ambles its way through post-industrial towns,
past fields of alfalfa blooms, past poplars

that have been there before, although you've never
sensed their sacredness. Let love be amazing.

And when the next station appears in full view,
all green tones and jazz tunes,

let two of these travelers disembark—
primed to begin their nights in pursuit.

The Idea of Ice Cream at Alki Beach

involves a responsive sweet cream text
dipped in external summer weather.

The idea of ice cream will engender pure elation—
(she licked the scoop as lovely as the sea).

It infuses rock salt magic with Greek myths
whorled with fig-tree honey.

Only a taste of dark chocolate and pistachio
will suffice for travelers from New England and Oman.

The idea of ice cream does not diminish over time
does not sing dripping each to each

but slowly thrums toward the oceanic divine—
indifferent to the tourist on the beach.

*

Is it time for the little truck to turn
toward the curbstone of our street?

We'd like to know. And soon.
Let's walk out and place our palms

above the silver sliding pane. Listen to
the gulls as the circus tune comes on

and we dream the eternal, hard refrain
of *mine, mine, mine.* We call and calling

make it so—the sundaes, rockets, and éclairs
we hold and in holding enact the American

ritual of joy—the tongue and all its vagrant tastes,
before we unfold the cloud-lit wrappers coast to coast.

Not a Still Life

She was most desirous of round things—
Roman glass, the texture of the sea.
Iridescent bowls, porcelain masks, zinnia in spring.
Paint colors: cinnamon, ochre, green. Things that shine:
white apples, survival, a strand of turquoise beads.
She coveted ginger jars, wooden clogs, one husband
(sometimes months unseen), cloudscapes, three katsura trees.
She'd meditate on Chemistry, Chinese art, her New York
magazines—bright stream of all she'd gleaned.
Among her skills: photography and psalms, how to mend
a heart, an evening dress, a career polished to a song.
Madeira, Algiers, Rhodes—the light different in each one.
But what she wanted most has all but disappeared.
The museum walls, the fame—the name not written here.

Hunger is the Best Cook

—after a photograph by Myra Albert Wiggins, 1898

Dark bowl, small mouth, sumptuous spoon—

Whatever there is
there's not much here,

but the girl's intent—

enraptured nearly—in the pause
and trick of it, the mythic

mirror of abeyance. Her body

opens toward the rim
of awe—all lick and swallow,

imagination readying the tongue.

* * *

Is art simply a hymn to reconfiguration:

Wild huckleberries,
wedge of bread, broken chaff

from the season's ripe wheat?

The museum patron
presumes the sharp taste—

believes fully in the meal

where the spoon doesn't waver—
where the girl will

never bring this moment to its end and eat—

* * *

But this is not the story

of the actual:
moon-faced, well-fed,

photographer's daughter

re-clothed and then
again, for a mother's ambitious narrative.

The costume, the curtains, the fable

rise in what the woman
called *The Vermeer Style*—

deficiency reshaped for pleasure's sake.

* * *

Fistfuls of wildflowers

rupture the room as she shoots
frame after frame

cajoling the unstudied studio pose.

Is her family shrapnel or daisy chain?
Wiggins' curved hand

charting the shutter: half-right, half-wrong—

lighting through to
the alchemist's kitchen—

Mr. Myra Albert Wiggins
Recalls Their Arrangement

Maybe it was the bicycle. The way her hips
rose up and up—as if directed straight to heaven—

Like a Venus. And a banker's daughter—true.
Real original, this girl—a bicycle, a camera,

other newfangled tools. I sent her bolts
of cloth, overalls, and boots—anything to make her squint

her eyes and glance one day towards me—me: Fred
Wiggins of Wiggins Bazaar—123 Commercial Street.

More of a back-up boyfriend, for someone like Myra
her family would say. Everyone knew she was in love

with her own life: bareback rides, opera singing,
and the New York *artiste* nights. But I expected

to live a little, too. And so if there were men
of Salem, Toppenish, Seattle, lovely and rich—

who snickered at our last-season suits
and sequined gowns, who hinted not infrequently—

that a husband should not be so happy
packing picture frames and mounting

photographs. Christ. They knew nothing.

Polishing Brass

Myra used her maid, Alma Schmidt, as a subject in several
of her pictorial photographs of Dutch domestic life. Schmidt
wore costumes and posed in a variety of theatrical scenes.
No further record of their relationship exists.

No, more a holy meditation
on surface and stain:

Madonna with Vessel.

The inland
glow of white shoulders

rivulet of vertebrae

vestige of one breath-
takingly long

and sexual arm
which grasps

the ledge
of the cauldron

as she curves onward.

       *

Remember form:

nothing more

than potent omen—

pyramid of saucepan top,
overflow

of water bucket,
angle of the invisible skin—

dimpled underneath her garment—

*

A light-stroked body,
conflicted as rosewater, as clotted cream—

*

Alma, grace of more
than poor

Our Lady of the Scullery Shimmer—

starlet of
returning questions

May I serve you?

*

Perhaps art as polish

    gloss of what the photograph

portends in voyeurism.

    An aperture, a flash

of the nakedly conscious eye—

        a part of and apart—

blessing identity until it blinds us.

*

Once, on a sunlit afternoon

    a maidservant, an ingénue,

        swept forward—

into what this moment you

        in Almeria, Soho, Barcelona—

          might admire, must revise—

                a woman's hands:
fingernails, blue.

Paradise Now at Highline College

The class argues about the end of the movie—did the bomb detonate?
They can't agree. They try out multiple meanings for white

light, two human eyes, the breakneck speed of Said's life;
his grief. The black ash of question marks begin to rise

reluctantly above their freshmen heads—the procrastinated
fall into inquiry; *But what's this got to do with me?*

I cry out *flashback, foreshadow,* hope to teach the world
through mise-en-scene—to watch students interrogate

their own thinking. They side so easily with the suicide
bomber, understand instinctively two best friends

toppled by geography, their familiar junkyard lives.
In class discussion, my students appear almost dreamy—

Can there be a film industry, without a country?
Intifada and *Mossad* lift off their tongues

with hard-won confidence; the glossary—their global gun.
On which edge of the checkpoint should they rely? Arab

or Israeli? The questions with new answers lead them on,
keep them fractured, shiftshape some through to another side.

Portrait with Lorca

Beneath her shirt pages turn,
climbing her shoulders. Images
rearrange her breasts, then the thin line

of clavicle highlighting her underwire
x: two satin cups, black straps. Beneath her
shirt, lives are being lived by other women

other men. Families acquire toddlers,
several gerbils, teens. Often the world
underneath her blouse takes precedence

over what happens at school.
And so when the leather binding
touches her belly, nestles near her hips,

flirts with a reference to a Lorca aperitif—
she can no longer fool the old professor
who has loved someone, or two.

And when the tests come back,
her examination notebook stamped
in almond skins, perfume, and candle wax—

the commentary simply says,
We all wear branches that we do not
have. Castanet! Castanet! Castanet!

The Lost

As the *Night of The Living Dead*
unreels before us in the dark
you whisper to me vignettes of film history
explain how the lost art of withdrawing
red velvet curtains had anticipated
the moment before the action,
introduced the cinematic show.
How a person's hands had to be constant
eagerly holding down, arranging
one movement over the other
in a meditation that involved
the whole body.
And how after years of pulling the fabric
up and down
one old man in Tennessee is left
with an art no one else living
knows or wants to learn.
You bemoan how the arcing
of wrists has been replaced by automation
how tonight it's levers and cranks
which undress our sci-fi screen.
This is the story of tragedy you tell me
while across the aisle people swallow ice
through plastic straws and tear into
gold-wrapped chocolate swans
oblivious to all we have lost.

The Never Born Comes of Age

All day you bubble into liquid pieces
like a bath's surface, like a showerhead
with its dial of tricks, its pulse.

All day you search for the baobab tree
and mangos, the dayglow
lizards—the leper ladies

who laugh with you from empty bowls.

Remember Sa-a, his name
which meant *the lucky one?* How hours
hunched like logs no one could move,

time mugging the coffee table, the ledge

of each boys' elbows? You'd hear
the brag of the new Toyota,
your lover shouting *ina kwana*, calling out—

Remember? The millet fields,
the Nigerian make-up
girls used to bleach their skin,

your neighbor, multi-lingual and soccer-stricken?

Remember Prince and Freak Out,
the pink of washboard roads,
fast sex without a condom—

and its predictable results?

Little biscuit, lemon peel,
pig tether—the fetus
that quickly followed, never showed.

Here's the praise song to the almost
child, almost mother, father
—*almost, almost, almost*—

And voilà, Habiba, our caretaker

the day you left and didn't know—
the crush of her wise body like a
waterfall, a levy overflowed.

Loss streaming across cow dung and thistle—
And still here, beside the bath, this ghost-child,
dragging waterproof alphabet, soggy cupcake, silent whistle.

Interview

Sarajevo, Bosnia and Herzegovina

In her mind, she needs to cross the boundary
navigate clear water, sleep again, be whole—
she'll erase her Muslim name, forget life's memory.

Why not Bavaria? Why not the travel remedy?
Study without the Sarajevo Rose.
Her mind a boat; she floats across the boundary.

Everyone said, *the conflict? only temporary*—
She'll call her family often; keep close by telephone;
pour the past away, skip the shit of memory.

But each night she pays, this is not her country.
The thoughts shoot back and forth, a mental palindrome.
Her mind: ocean without boundary.

Other students stare in disbelief as she leaves, quietly.
A homing instinct, streams; she charts the map alone.
Is the past no more than present memory?

For one moment, her return is almost celebratory.
Mortar rounds and shelling, a kind of pleasure dome.
Her mind circles round blue boundaries.

Letter to the End of the Year

Lately, I am capable of small things.

Peeling an orange.
Drawing a bath.
Throwing the cat's tinsel ball.

Believe me, this is not unhappiness.

Only one question—
why this layering on of abeyance?

Though it is winter inside of me—

there is also spring and fall.

Yellow tulips in need of planting
root in a basket by the door.

Tonight, mortality seems cloistered in a pinecone

close-windowed, remote.

What was the peak moment
of your happiness?

And how did you know?

For weeks, it's been oatmeal,
the Internet, an Irish shawl.

I realize, I am growing older
and stranger.

Please, don't misunderstand.

I am still impatient
still waiting for symbiant and swoon

the litter of blue-gold—

a one-time constellation:

Now, before you go.

Unexpected Song

Thank-you for sending me back
to the page, the open notebook,

Duende's unfurled tail
along the table's edge.

Thank-you for apricot blossoms,
beach rose and blackberry vines

that allow bright divinations
along the nearly absent mind.

And hats off to the green
and white ferries over-riding

timetables, taxes, spring tides;
to the brants' triumphant choir

casually premiering each April
along the waters of Beach Drive,

above Vashon, Bainbridge, Blake,
like a flyway to the heart.

Outside this raised window
lay early morning charms

traveling the air on blue lilac—
terrestrial and round:

the notes we are meant to sing
the possibility in each slight thing.

Facing 50 with a Line by Robert Hayden

There is so much that clings to us—
not just cat fur and grass

seed, but also chocolate

creams and the white beach
of childhood, an extended sash of blue.

     *

Not just sadness and solace,

but what the body
reveals after waking,

the open heart and a watery

sense of who we are, the life we attempted to choose.

     *

What clings to us (train trips, questions)
fall forward to all

the future will randomly

reduce to an email, an hour,
a knot of pleasure—nearly pursued.

     *

The seasons clock on

decorating the light we crave
like a dim-sum tray—

rich, sensual, and brand new

to each other—

*

as Shakespearean fools, as Pomeranians,

a bright pair of trusted boots.

from
CLOUD PHARMACY
(2014)

Blue Grapes

There were days made entirely of dust
months of counter-winds

      and years unbalanced on the windowsill.

The soup poured in the same yellowed cup.

Newspapers appeared like oracles on your doorstep—gilded fragments
of anonymous love.

      You stayed in bed, read novels, drank too much.

God visited, delivered ice cream; returned your delinquent library books.

Is it simpler after you're dead
to watch the living like characters on an old TV set?

      The dying are such acrobats—

you see them ringing doorbells with their clipboards
remarking on the globes of lilacs.

      They try to lure you out; request a drink of water,
some blue grapes. This does not work.

      Then the dying leave you to yourself—

to the girl dressed in black, suffused with commas,
and question marks——

      How to write your one blue life?

Tricks a Girl Can Do

*Hannah Maynard was one of the first professional women photographers
in Victoria, British Columbia. After the death of her teenage daughter,
Lillie, she created a series of multiple exposure self-portraits. From 1884
to 1896, Maynard's work grew progressively eccentric.*

I will hang myself in picture frames
in drawing rooms where grief
is not allowed a wicker chair

then grimace back at this façade
from umbrella eyes,
through a cage of silvering hair.

Look! I've learned to slice myself in three
to sit politely at the table
with ginger punch and teacake,

to offer thin-lipped graves
of pleasantries. I develop myself
in the pharmacist's chemicals

three women I'm loathed to understand—
presences I sometimes cajole
into porcelain light and shadow.

We culminate in a silver gelatin scene—
a daughter birthed from a spiral shell,
a keyhole tall enough to strut through.

Childhood Study: Fires Late August

Awake in the middle of the night,
we listen to the grass crackle, to the new world of evacuate.

Like monkeys we screech as the trees go pop—

yellow candelabras, we see and then not.
Now danger damages our capillaries

for the first time, the ladder trucks and sirens

seem like small toys compared
with the neighbor's fire-fangled trees.

What lit-up between us that summer—

three sisters clustered like barn cats—I can't say
except for a time camaraderie

warmed the soles of our feet, our robes

remaining intact just one season—
before it burned away.

Dear Self

The word I object to in the poem is blue
as in aquamarine, periwinkle, cornflower;

the shade of rain, of wind, of a girl's bicycle
stolen from the beach last July. I object

to the semi-colon; the commonplace
comma, the em dash—as in Blue Danube—

blue fool—the sheen of a junkyard cat.

I object to the monogamous couplet

the iambic flash,   the turn
in the line like a magician who displays his jackrabbit—

sheer entertainment done strictly for cash.
I abhor the smooth paper, the *vision fine* pen,

the hand mixing the ink, yes even the author
who praises acres of tulips, orgasms in France.

Tunnel

The wind blows through
the chain linked yards of Allston Street.

   It lifts the neighbor's forsythia into a Ferris wheel

of light and tips the girl aloft for the first time.

Now the petals follow her
along the cellar stairs in a yellow yelp

of March, passing the candy dish, filled
to overflowing by invisible hands—

ominous Bullseyes, endless M&M's;
to the first-floor tenants newly married;

the glamorous man with a green anchor
on his arm

     re-names her "pea-nut" and drives diesel trucks
which excites the child, tremendously.

    In the wind tunnel, now their living room,

the couple talk as if they live
among horses and lobsterpots.
           As they embrace her,

she knows this as the encyclopedia

of her real world. The life of undershirts
and pipe smoke,

penny candy. Love so fresh it appears
palpable.

The wind of her heart now

follows her up more stairs to the other mother,
other father, then drifts down

hallways so grim it seems as if an aunt in Cincinnati
has just died

and then nine cousins drowned, too.

    The wind follows her through the attic of the dead
    where she touches their beautiful

chins with her thumb. It is peaceful here

when she walks through herself
                    leaning above the current's edge.

American History

Someday soon I'll be saying, at school

there were chalkboards, at school
we read books made of paper,

we drank milk from small cartons. We drew.
At school we met children unlike us,

studied evolution, enjoyed recess, plenty of food.

At school we made globes of papier-mâché,
built solar systems democratized in sugar cubes.

At school we sang harmonies of Lennon-
McCartney, we were cool;

collected pennies for children in
Biafra, Bangladesh, and Timbuktu.

There were teachers of Plato, King,
and Kennedy, all paid for by taxpayers

supporting an ordinary American school.

Sugar, You Know Who You Are

You who carry the sky in your hands
open to the world as peach pie;

you who harmonize like a Miracle,
a Temptation, a Spinner, a Top—

What record shop or percussive bop
did you swing from? What city

plot did you rhythmically cajole
of a singer making music to a woman—

not young, not yet so old! Remember?
We watched ourselves

as if watching strangers improvise
a summer's afternoon

composed from the riff of madrona
leaves, iced coffee, and a public wading pool.

Maybe we were beginning
our lives together, maybe.

The hinges squeaked
a kind of jazz tune—coconut bars

and jelly rolls, Boston egg creams,
and red velvet stars. No longer

strangers now, the blue gates open
at dusk and look

here you are: infusing the globe
in rhythms, sugaring our nights with sparks.

You Who No Longer Concern Me

I revise the canvas of our under-painted sky.

Move the shoreline backwards until blank.
But how to erase the island countries,

the sea-filled nights, your love sighs more

addictive than cheap flights? I am tired
so tired of small fights, the sleepless pacing, waking

the cat up, the damned neighbors, the fucking

flies. I am ready for another life: blue
lawn afternoons with roundtable friends—

jasmine, mint cocktails, a full vegetable bed.

You who no longer concern me, you are
the unread novel, the half-closed eye, the rubato

of trains in this city's west section.

And if you were to ask me now
with shimmering bees, scat filmstrip

jazz and endnote: *Will you be mine?*

I do not believe that it would be enough—
but you may try to right our lives again.

You may try, but I am unconcerned.

Dutch Courtyard

She labors but at what she cannot know for sure.
She is alone but does she know

how she's observed? The outer wall, the window
where girls of ivory and rose watch knowingly

above a makeshift fence; they can't
foresee the story of her winged back, know

nothing of the image-maker's script, the color work—
her supporting bit as laundress, lover, know-

it-all in service to the day's grey socks. Her face remains
defiantly obscured. What can she know

of art? She is arms—green bucket—angled foot—
headscarf—house dress—body of a woman. Knowledge

that she would most likely like to wash away—what good will it do her?
Blue motion of her life elevated to nowhere.

She's judged simple, dirty, ugly—and maybe so.
But see this future person standing here, knowing

all she does of sorrow, bend to palm the frame,
stung by something the world cannot express: the notion

of a second soul. She journeys in, traveling by window—
worker, rich girl, artist in the street: go beyond the known.

Hannah, Decanter, and Cloud

Age is still decanters on the table
the size of small chandeliers
or cloud foam. You, remember,
are the one that is unmade
as of yet, unknown. Medium
merely to an image, a woman

studio-posed. Self-portrait
developed for the afterlife—
our ticker-tape world

of tableaus and combs
circling on. And. Then. Somehow
your barnacled vessel
lit from within like a carriage
clock or sea-washed amber stones.
Have you been taken?

The Victorians inquired; from flesh
into silver salts, into gaslight paper
or gold? Everyone becoming older.

Your gaze darts forward, lifts
beyond the mayor's clapperboard
home, the dead dove, the séance, the bones.
One unknowable instant—
even as the aperture quietly
holds, even as the light

decants over gloved hands
that turn into clouds.
Don't tell me this is only a story.

Tell me there's more to our lives
than jigsaws and doorknobs,
more than tumbleweed, sediment or sex.
We live for the tunnel, the years signatured
together into the surreal, for our art
imperfect and striving.

In a Village West of Galway

A woman takes her place
at the desk, a Moleskine open
before her like an eye.

She works, she pays, she cajoles
observation, determined to learn
the lighthouse within her—

and lead it to the page.
Yet how to transcribe
this invisible boundary line—

both lucid and in shadow;
to know her life? And to step outside.
Linger where the debris

of language, unmoored,
accumulates as local bird
song, kite string, tossed-away

paradox. Her mind
navigates only this much—
images accumulate like buttons

in a button jar; needled
and threaded. Suspended—
she closes the journal, the world, the vastness—

tilt-a-whirls herself into the laundry
and lunchboxes. Cooking oil heating
from early-morning food stalls,

last evening's rain on pine needles,
cloudscapes that slip from lavender
into grey. Tomorrow she will

reattach herself, line by line-
break to this radiant quarrel,
this pocket-sized, revolutionary pen.

Cloud Pharmacy

How many apothecary drawers
could I fill with these deliberations?

The pharmacist's paper cone
parsing out a quarter cup

of love's resistant drug,
spoons measuring new prescriptions

for my uncertainty, heartsway, gesture.
Give me cobalt bottles

leftover from Aunt Iska's cures,
albastrons of ointments, resins to resolve

the double-helix of desire inside of me.
Where is the votive, the vessel,

the slide rule calculation
of how much good love

alchemically speaking
is good enough?

I want spindrift nights on swimmer's
thighs. I want an Egyptian

elevator inlaid in camphorwood and ivory;
a West African drumbeat, an eggnog, a god.

I want waves and summer all year long.
I want you. And I want more.

Going—

Until one has loved an animal, a part of one's soul remains unawakened.

—Anatole France

I photograph you every morning
In a cruel attempt to capture
A formal souvenir of what I love
After breakfast, and then
Each day a little less
You take a stand, examine finches
Windowpanes knocking
Your head against my hand
Until you don't—
There is no way to tell you
That you are going
With few days left
For what our rebel hearts relay

Faraway

I like it here in the green Beara chair
the Wellington boots

      perched in pairs beneath the kitchen window.

I like the palm trees so clearly out of place,

the Irish cow's peculiar baritone keening

like a mobile phone
         on pulse.

I like it here because the peninsula is curved and long,

the road edged in orange wildflowers and dung.

I like how the clouds put on a juried show
         and the rain.

That here the interior world opens
lightly as a letter

with no sentences of sorrow.

The World to Come

Let's say we make our own happiness, roll over in the fields,
stain our arms and legs with blue

grass; let's say there's simply one year left
to draw lists of clouds, slip guilt-free through bars

of chocolate, hold each other in this black hole
of restlessness. This life.

Tonight we will battle the linoleum squares,
laundry stairs, glass deck where one day

the body is sure to grab its last hungry breath.
What if all that's left for us is gravity,

canned soup, a shimmer of thinning hair?
Let's say we make our own happiness, even so—

the tail swoop of katsura trees, triple shots
of strong coffee, a folded map—

Then may I remember to thank the academy
of daily minutiae: suitcases, car keys, a friend's

first novel of karaoke. Who says we can't
have it all: the house of sky and soft catcalls—

Who says we can't find another way
to fail, to come up short, to catch and release.

Acknowledgements & Thanks

A bazillion and one thanks to all the people, organizations, and angels that have come together to help me in the creation of this book. I could not have done it without you. A book such as this is a collage of lived experience which happens in community, in connection with others.

For giving her time and expertise with a consummate kindness, I am forever thankful to Katherine Flenniken. For close readings on individual poems and overall crucial writing and life support, thank you to Kelli Russell Agodon and Elizabeth Austen. For transatlantic packages and wide support since the beginning, thank you to Geraldine Mills. Thank you to Mark Doty for advice on this new and selected idea, curated during wildfire season!

For my writing group that understands that revision and good food go hand in hand: deep gratitude to Chris Balk, Michelle Bombardier, Suzanne Edison, Katie Ellis, Susan Landgraf, Martha Silano, Anne Teplick and Cindy Veach. For long walks and longer talks, thank you to Claudia Castro Luna and Laura Urban Perry. For late-night phone calls and literary dreams, thanks to January Gill O'Neil. And thank you to Gina Formea for an entire wheelhouse of support.

Heartfelt thanks to the many organizations and foundations that have supported the creation of this work: Artists Trust, 4 Culture, Blue Mountain Center, Centrum, CityArtists, Hedgebrook, Helene Whitely Center, Jack Straw Writers, Millay Arts, Ucross Foundation, Helene Wurlitzer Foundation, Tyrone Guthrie Center and the Highline College Professional Leave Program. A special thank you and profound gratitude to Dr. John Mosby, who believes in the power of poetry to edify, empower, and offer students creative pathways to reach their highest potential through the alchemy of words.

1001 hurrahs to the Poets on the Coast sisters, you sustain and uplift me. The literary community we have developed together is the kindest and most generous I've known. Deep bow most especially to Sandy Yaonne. To my travel companion from Ireland to Morocco, from Italy to places not yet found on any map, heartfelt gratitude to Angie Vorhies.

Thank you to Ruby Rich and Mary Peelen for familial love, support and real friendship.

Finally, to Jessie Lendennie and Siobhán Hutson, profound thanks for the all-important and sustaining work that you do for poetry in Ireland, and internationally.

Thank you to the estate of Remedios Varo and the Artists Rights Society for one-time non-exclusive English language worldwide rights for the use of the painting, "Caravan, 1955".

Heartfelt thanks to the poetry editors and staff of the journals where these poems first appeared, often in slightly different forms.

Caravan of Doves

JOURNALS:
Blackbird Journal: "What I Learned from *Bewitched*"
Box of Matches: "Self Portrait as a Leonora Carrington Painting"
Cold Mountain Review: "Two vegetarian vampires walk into a bar"
Crannóg Magazine: "Every Clock is Made of Foxes;" "Someday I Will Love Susan Rich"
Guesthouse: "First Knowledge"
Helen Literary Magazine: "Pomegranate, Radio On— "
Image Journal: "Tonight, I Travel Back to Allston Street"
Missouri Review: "A 99-Year-Old Woman Wakes to Find"
Naugatuck River Review: "Physics of Causality"
Pangyrus Journal: "Song at the End of the Mind"
Pleiades: 'Self Portrait with Stained Glass and Feathers"
Plume: "Secret Agent," 'The Giantess'
Radar Poetry: "How to Travel in the Middle Period"
River Mouth Review: "Tired of Being a Woman"
Solstice: A Magazine of Diverse Voices: "Dear Wild Unknown"
Sugar House Review: "Self Portrait as Gustav Courbet"
Tar River Poetry: "You Might Be Wondering Why I Called You Here"
The Sea Wall: "Elegy for Grace"
Women's Quarterly: "True Story"

ANTHOLOGIES:
"Song at the End of the Mind," Jennifer Haupt, ed., *Alone Together*, Central Avenue Publishing, BC, Canada, 2020

MULTIMEDIA PROJECTS:
"We Wish to Name It, That's What Humans Do," is part of the *Telephone 2020 Project*, the largest collaborative art project in the world dreamed-up and co-designed by Nathan Langston. The poem was inspired by a photographic work by Casey Kelbaugh.

The four previous books of poems, *Cloud Pharmacy*, *The Alchemist's Kitchen*, *Cures Include Travel*, and *The Cartographer's Tongue/Poems of the World* were all published by White Pine Press. Grateful acknowledgements are also due to the journals where many of these poems first appeared.

Grateful acknowledgments to the following journals where these poems first appeared, often in earlier versions. Sincere thanks to the editors for their belief in my work. *Bellingham Review*: "Flightpath." *Clackamas Review*: "Photograph, May 10th 1939." *Cranky*: "On the Corner of Washington and 3rd." *North American Review*: "The Dead Eat Blueberry Scones for Breakfast." *Salamander*: "What She Leaves Unspoken." *Poetry International*: "Mohamud at the Mosque," "The Women of Kismayo." *Sojourner Prize*: "Everyone in Bosnia Loves Begonias." Natural Bridge: "Change," Witness, "Fissure."

Grateful acknowledgments to the following journals where these poems first appeared, often in earlier versions. Sincere thanks to the editors for their belief in my work. *Antioch Review*: "The Never Born Comes of Age." Art Access: "Unexpected Song." *Bellevue Literary Review*: "Transcendence." *Crab Creek Review*: "Not a Still Life." *Harvard Review*: "Interview." *New England Review*: "At Middle Life: A Romance." *Notre Dame Review*: "Tulip Sutra." Poet Lore: "Dear Self." *Poetry International*: "Food for Fallen Angels." *The Southern Review*: "Mr. Myra Albert Wiggins Recalls Their Arrangement." *Third Coast*: "Hunger is the Best Cook." *Times Literary Supplement* (London): "Different Places to Pray." *TriQuarterly*: "Letter to the End of the Year."

Acknowledgments to the following journals where these poems first appeared, often in slightly different versions. *Alaska Quarterly Review*: "Tunnel." *Bellingham Review*: "Blue Grapes," "Sugar, You Know Who You Are." *CascadiaChronicle.com*: "Dutch Courtyard." City Arts: "Cloud Pharmacy." *Crab Creek Review*: "Tricks a Girl Can Do." *Life Study*: "Fires Late August." *Hollins Critic Review*: "Faraway Kestrel: In a Village West of Galway." *New England Review*: "The World to Come." Poet Lore: "Dear Self." *Southern Review*: "Going—." *Syracuse Cultural Workers' Calendar*: "You Who No Longer Concern Me."

Notes & Dedications

Caravan of Doves

"Pomegranate, Radio On" is dedicated to poet and mentor, Madeline DeFrees.

"Secret Agent" is for Leonora Carrington, the inspiration comes from her painting, *The Old Maids.*

"Caravan of One" is inspired by the painting and cover art, *Caravan*, 1958, by Remedios Varo.

"Elegy For Grace" is dedicated to Grace Jones, mother to Paul & Deb, grandmother to Becky & Ellie.

"Extreme Close-Up" takes initial inspiration from *American Sonnets for My Past and Future Assassin*, by Terrance Hayes, Penguin, 2019.

"Self Portrait as Leonora Carrington" borrows inspiration from *Self Portrait c. 1937*, by Leonora Carrington.

"Reading the Rising Tides" borrows the line from Rilke, 'Against so strong a current you cannot advance.'

"Remedios" takes inspiration from *Exploring the Sources of the Orinoco River*, 1959, by Remedios Varo.

"Night Windows Above the Street" is after Edward Hopper's, *Night Windows*, 1928.

"Vegetarian Vampires walk into a bar" is inspired by *Vegetarian Vampires*, 1962 by Remedios Varo.

"Someday I Will Love Susan Rich" is after the poem by Roger Reeves, "Someday I Will Love Roger Reeves" from his collection, *King Me*, Copper Canyon Press, 2013. This poem was in response to Frank O'Hara's poem, "Katie" which includes the lines, "Someday, Someday I'll love Frank O'Hara. / I think I'll be alone for a little while."

"99-Year-Old Woman Wakes to Find" is inspired by a news story in the *Miami Herald*, January 26, 2016: "99-Year-Old Woman Wakes Up to Find Exotic Animal on Her Chest."

"Tired of Being a Woman" takes initial inspiration from Pablo Neruda's poem "Tired of Being a Man."

"How to Travel in the Middle Period" is for Angie Vorhies.

The Cartographer's Tongue / Poems of the World

"Oslobođenje": *Oslobođenje,* Sarajevo's independent newspaper published every day during the three and a half years of the Bosnian war. *Oslobođenje*'s offices were targeted and set alight by Serbian forces during the first three months of the seige. The poem is based on an interview with Kemal Kurspahić published in the *American Scholar,* Spring 1998.

"Whatever Happened to the Bodies": The poem was inspired by a National Public Radio story aired on March 10, 1996, which began "This evening we bring you a report about an unusual, grim, and sacred perspective on the recent bombings. We join the Volunteers who help clean up the carnage. Jewish law states it's a special Mitzvah to bring a body, to bury it whole, to give it the best respect.

Cures Include Travel

"Mohamud at the Mosque" is dedicated to Mohamud Esmail; first student, then brother.

"A Poem for Will, Baking" is dedicated to Rabbi Will Berkovitz

"Not a Prayer" is in memory of my mother, Lillian Rich (1921-1995).

"Unexpected Song" is for Peter Aaron

The Alchemist's Kitchen

"Tulip Sutra" is for Mustafa and Reyyan Bal.

"Portrait with Lorca" borrows its last two lines from Lorca.

"Interview" is for Larisa Kasumagić, Sarajevo, Bosnia and Herzegovina. The poem references the Sarajevo Rose: the pattern made by a mortar shell exploding; specifically, it refers to the imprint left on the tarmac.

Myra Albert Wiggins (1869-1956) was born in Salem, Oregon; she was the first Northwest woman photographer to achieve high acclaim for her work and exhibit her pictures nationally and internationally in the company of Alfred Stieglitz, Edward J. Steichen, and others.

The Wiggins' poems owe a great debt to *The Witch of Kodakery The Photography of Myra Albert Wiggins 1869-1956*, by Carole Gauber, published by Washington State University Press,1997, which informed and often jump-started the poems. "Hunger is the Best Cook" and "Polishing Brass" borrow titles from the photographs which inspired them. "Mr. Myra Albert Wiggins Considers Their Arrangement" and "Not a Still Life" are non-photographic imaginings of Wiggins' life story.

"Blue Grapes" borrows the line, "the dying are such acrobats" from *Trapeze* by Deborah Digges.

"Sugar, You Know Who You Are" is dedicated to Jeff Wasserman.

"Dutch Courtyard" is after *Courtyard*, c.1884, by Max Liebermann, in the Founders' Collection of the Frye Art Museum, Seattle, WA

Hannah Maynard (1834-1918) was born in Cornwall, England, and immigrated with her husband, Richard, to Canada, eventually settling in Victoria, B.C., in 1862. From the late 1880's to the 1890's, Maynard created a series of self-portraits experimenting with multiple exposure and trick photography shots. These multiple exposure self-portraits and other proto-surreal pieces are the photographs referenced in the poems. Thanks to Claire Weissman Wilks for her book, *The Magic Box—The Eccentric Genius of Hannah Maynard* (Exile Editions, 1980).

"Faraway" is dedicated to the poets and writers in residence at Anam Cara in the West of Ireland—past, present, and future.

Photo credit: Kristie McLean

SUSAN RICH is the author of four previous poetry collections, including *Cloud Pharmacy*, *The Alchemist's Kitchen*, named a finalist for the Forward Prize and the Washington State Book Award, *Cures Include Travel*, and *The Cartographer's Tongue*, winner of the PEN USA Award and the Peace Corps Writers Prize (White Pine Press).

She co-edited *The Strangest of Theatres: Poets Writing Across Borders* (McSweeneys). Her poems and essays have been published in seven different countries.

Rich has received awards and fellowships from Fulbright Foundation, PEN USA, The Times Literary Supplement of London, Peace Corps Writers, Artist Trust, CityArtists, and 4Culture.

She has worked as a staff person for Amnesty International, an electoral supervisor in Bosnia and Herzegovina, and a human rights trainer in Gaza and the West Bank. Rich lived in the Republic of Niger, West Africa as a Peace Corps Volunteer, later moving to South Africa to teach at the University of Cape Town on a Fulbright Fellowship. Her awards include: the Times (London) Literary Supplement Award, a residency at the Tyrone Guthrie Center in Ireland and a residency at Fundacion Valparaiso in Spain. Other poetry honors include an Artist Trust Fellowship, 4 Culture Awards, a Seattle CityArtist Project Award, GAP Awards, and participation in the Cúirt Literary Festival in Galway, Ireland.

Rich is an alumna of Hedgebrook, the Helen Whiteley Center, Millay Colony for the Arts, and the Ucross Foundation. She has served on the boards of Crab Creek Review, Floating Bridge Press and Whit Press. Educated at the University of Massachusetts, Harvard University, and the University of Oregon, Susan Rich lives in Seattle and teaches at Highline College where she runs the reading series, Highline Listens: Writers Read Their Work. She is co-founder and director of Poets on the Coast: A Weekend Writing Retreat for Women. More information is easily accessed at www.poetsusanrich.com

salmonpoetry

Cliffs of Moher, County Clare, Ireland

"Publishing the finest Irish and international literature."
Michael D. Higgins, President of Ireland